GW01032680

Our Good Provider

Delighting in God's Gifts

Six Studies for Groups or Individuals
with Notes for Leaders

Lin Johnson

Foreword by J. I. Packer

Inter-Varsity Press

INTER-VARSITY PRESS
38 De Montfort Street, Leicester LE1 7GP, England

OUR GOOD PROVIDER: *Delighting in God's Gifts*
Copyright © 1994 by Lin Johnson

First published in the USA by Zondervan Publishing House in 1994

First British edition 1995

British Library Cataloguing in Publication Data

A catalogue record for this book is available from the British Library.

ISBN 0-85111-350-8

Typeset and printed in the United States of America

Inter-Varsity Press is the book-publishing division of the Universities and Colleges Christian Fellowship (formerly the Inter-Varsity Fellowship), a student movement linking Christian Unions in universities and colleges throughout the United Kingdom and the Republic of Ireland and a member movement of the International Fellowship of Evangelical Students. For information about local and national activities write to UCCF, 38 De Montfort Street, Leicester LE1 7GP.

95 96 97 98 99 00 /DP/ 6 5 4 3 2 1

Contents

Foreword

One big difference between our current culture and that of a century ago is that the Victorians saw life in terms of roles, while we see it in terms of relationships. Real life, we say, is a matter of relationships, for roles minimize personal involvement while relationships maximize it.

In saying this, we speak more Christian truth than perhaps we realize. For real life according to the Bible means relating not just to other people but also to the personal God who made us. We live and move and exist in him, and it is both scandalous and impoverishing when we ignore him.

Who is he? The startling truth is that he is a *society*. The Father, Son, and Holy Spirit share with each other an intimate and loving relationship. Yet in the unity of their interpersonal life, they constitute a single divine being. God is they, a society and a team, and they are he, the only God there is.

A mystery? An inexplicable reality? Yes, but a life-giving one. It is our privilege not simply to acknowledge the truth of the Trinity but also to enter into Spirit-sustained relationship with the Father and the Son—a relationship which from one standpoint is *eternal life*, and from another is *knowing God*.

Knowing people involves, first, knowing facts about them and, second, making their acquaintance. How deep our relationship goes depends on how much empathy we have, how many concerns and interests we share, and how much we seek to exalt the one we love. It is the same with knowing God.

The Bible is God's communication to all who hear or read it. Through its varied contents the Triune Lord tells us about himself and calls us to himself. A proper understanding of the Bible will focus at every point on both the information about God and the invitation to know him.

Knowing God Bible Studies are designed to help you achieve this focus. I heartily recommend them. They generate vision, insight, wisdom, and devotion in equal quantities. Use them and you will be blessed.

J. I. Packer

Knowing God Bible Studies

Every Christian desires a deeper, more personal relationship with God. We long to know him better, to feel his presence, and to experience his power in our lives. Jesus himself tells us, "This is eternal life: that they may know you, the only true God, and Jesus Christ, whom you have sent" (John 17:3).

Knowing God Bible Studies can help you build greater intimacy with God. The series explores who God is and how you can know him better. Each guide focuses on a specific attribute of God, such as his love, his faithfulness, or his mercy. The studies are warm and practical and personal—yet they are firmly grounded in Scripture.

The Knowing God series has been field tested in churches across America, representing a wide variety of denominations. This time-intensive process ensures that the guides have solid biblical content, consistent quality, easy-to-use formats, and helpful leader's notes.

Knowing God Bible Studies are designed to be flexible. You can use the guides in any order that is best for you or your group. They are ideal for Sunday-school classes, small groups, one-on-one relationships, or as materials for your quiet times.

Because each guide contains only six studies, you can easily explore more than one attribute of God. In a Sunday-school class, any two guides can be combined for a quarter (twelve weeks), or the entire series can be covered in a year.

Each study deliberately focuses on a limited number of passages, usually only one or two. That allows you to see each passage in its context, avoiding the temptation of prooftexting and the frustration of "Bible hopscotch" (jumping from verse to verse). If you would like to look up additional passages, a Bible concordance will give the most help.

Knowing God Bible Studies help you *discover* what the Bible says rather than simply *telling* you the answers. The questions encourage you to think and to explore options rather than merely to fill in the blanks with one-word answers.

Leader's notes are provided in the back of each guide. They show how to lead a group discussion, provide additional information on questions, and suggest ways to deal with problems that may come up in the discussion. With such helps, someone with little or no experience can lead an effective study.

SUGGESTIONS FOR INDIVIDUAL STUDY

1. Begin each study with prayer. Ask God to help you understand the passage and to apply it to your life.

2. A good modern translation, such as the *New International Version*, the *New American Standard Bible*, or the *New Revised Standard Version*, will give you the most help. Questions in this guide, however, are based on the *New International Version*.

3. Read and reread the passage(s). You must know what the passage says before you can understand what it means and how it applies to you.

4. Write your answers in the space provided in the study guide. This will help you to clearly express your understanding of the passage.

5. Keep a Bible dictionary handy. Use it to look up any unfamiliar words, names, or places.

SUGGESTIONS FOR GROUP STUDY

1. Come to the study prepared. Careful preparation will greatly enrich your time in group discussion.

2. Be willing to join in the discussion. The leader of the group will not be lecturing but will encourage people to discuss what they have learned in the passage. Plan to share what God has taught you in your individual study.

3. Stick to the passage being studied. Base your answers on the verses being discussed rather than on outside authorities such as commentaries or your favorite author or speaker.

4. Try to be sensitive to the other members of the group. Listen attentively when they speak, and be affirming whenever you can. This will encourage more hesitant members of the group to participate.

5. Be careful not to dominate the discussion. By all means participate! But allow others to have equal time.

6. If you are the discussion leader, you will find additional suggestions and helpful ideas in the leader's notes at the back of the guide.

Introducing Our Good Provider

When I had surgery two years ago—without paid sick days—I couldn't work for six weeks and then only half days for another six weeks. During that time, I experienced God's good provisions in abundance. Friends performed mundane tasks like grocery shopping, banking, and vacuuming. People from my congregation provided individual frozen meals I could pop into the microwave. Someone sent a $600 anonymous money order, the exact amount I needed to finish paying my bills one month. God had provided miraculously.

At one point, when I desperately needed money, I came home to find a box of food tailored to my special diet needs in front of the door. Two days later, I found an envelope with several hundred-dollar bills inside. God had provided miraculously.

God doesn't always meet my needs in such spectacular ways. But writing the mortgage check each month reminds me that he provides enough income to keep my condo. Meetings with my accountability and prayer partner focus my attention on how God provides strength, power, and spiritual growth. And the sharing time in my congregation's worship services allows me to declare God's benefits and works during the past week and to hear how much he has provided for others.

When pressures, bills, disappointments, and lack of sleep bury me, I look forward to God's ultimate gift of eternity with him when I'll never have to deal with these things again.

Certainly, God has provided abundantly for each of us. But too often we're so caught up in the dailyness of life that we don't stop to reflect on God and his provisions or to adequately praise and thank him.

This guide is designed to help correct that condition. The six studies introduce you to a variety of the Lord's good gifts, some of which you may have taken for granted or not thought about much. As you meet God in his role of Provider, ask him to make you more aware of what he does for you and more grateful for his gifts, since he "richly provides us with everything for our enjoyment" (1 Tim. 6:17).

Lin Johnson

1

Remembering God's Goodness

Psalm 103

Every spring, as they have for thousands of years, Jewish people celebrate Passover. They participate in a special service that recounts the Israelites' lives as slaves in Egypt, the ten plagues God sent on the Egyptians, and the miraculous exodus from Egypt. The story is illustrated with special foods, and everyone participates in the reading. Some of the customs in the modern service originated with early Jewish Christians to symbolize Christ's death as the Passover lamb and his resurrection—gifts from God worth remembering.

Participating in a Passover seder (service and meal) is a marvelous sensory experience to remember God's gift of physical redemption from Egypt. Messianic versions of Passover (led by Jewish people who believe Jesus is the promised Messiah) include verbal reminders of how God redeemed us spiritually from sin. The Lord's Supper, an abbreviated version of the Passover meal Jesus ate with his disciples before his death, serves as a similar reminder.

Whether or not we rely on special celebrations to remember God's gifts, Psalm 103 urges us to recall his goodness to us regularly.

1. What are some memorable gifts you have received?

Silk Sq.

Car (The Rover)

Why do you still remember them?

Special ones. - 1st gift -
Mother's criticism silenced -

2. Read Psalm 103. David begins this psalm with a call to praise, directed at himself. What do you learn about praise from verses 1–2?

We are grateful -

3. For what personal benefits does David praise God (vv. 3–5)?

forgiveness: healing : redemption
from the pit (sheol?)
love & mercy , desire satisfied

Why do you think he begins with the benefit of forgiveness?

1st necessity before any relationship
w. God can progress .

4. Select two or three benefits from the previous list, and describe briefly how you have experienced each one.

forgiveness - recently - for mother - relationship - desire - fulfilled life

5. What does David see in God's actions and character that are worthy of praise (vv. 6–10)?

supports the oppressed: helped the patriachs slow to anger - does not treat us as our sins deserve -

6. In verses 11–13, David uses three similes (comparisons that begin with the word as or like) to describe God's love and compassion. What are they, and what do they teach you about the Lord?

heaven above earth : his love east is from west : so far removed sins from us as father pities children : Lord has compassion on his children

7. How do you respond to this portrait of God's love, forgiveness, and compassion? Why?

Respond - gratitude - (seen human responses - marvel at God's)

8. What does God know about his children that makes him feel compassion (vv. 14–16)?

we are feeble & short - lived

How does our condition contrast with the Lord's love and
kingly rule (vv. 17–19)?

We are not constant - we have to be penitent -

9. What have you learned about God in this psalm that
makes you want to praise him?

His love & forgiveness in spite of all

What have you learned about yourself?

*Need to keep returning - confessing
praising*

10. Whom does David invite to join his celebration of praise
(vv. 20–22)? *Angels etc, heavenly hosts
& who obey God.
All God's creation.*

11. Spend a few minutes praising God for his goodness,
righteousness, forgiveness, compassion, and love. As you
praise him, be aware of the fact that countless others in
heaven and on earth are joining with you in worshiping
the Lord.

Memory Verse

"Praise the LORD, O my soul; all my inmost being, praise his holy name. Praise the LORD, O my soul, and forget not all his benefits."

Psalm 103:1–2

BETWEEN STUDIES

Each day list five to ten of God's benefits that you have experienced. Then praise God for them. To get you started, you may want to do an alphabet listing, identifying benefits by the letters of the alphabet.

a) advice

b) benefits

c) care

d)

e) enable

2

Why We Shouldn't Worry

Matthew 6:25-34

When George Müller opened his orphanages in England in the 1800s, he continued a previous commitment to live by faith alone. Instead of talking to friends or writing prayer letters detailing the needs for money and food, he prayed. Often there was no food to feed the children and no money to buy what they needed. But Müller was not worried. He and the children trusted God to take care of their needs. More than once, they sat down for dinner with little or no food and thanked God for what he would provide. By the time they finished praying, a knock on the door brought an immediate answer. Although Müller never appealed for money, two thousand children always had food and proper clothing, and all debts were paid.

For many believers, George Müller's experiences resemble scenes from a fantasy movie. Instead of praying with the kind of faith he had, we tend to worry about our needs and try to meet them in our own strength. But God says there's a better way, as Matthew 6 reveals.

1. Think of a time when you prayed for something you needed that you couldn't afford instead of charging it or worrying about it. How did God answer your prayer?

2. Read Matthew 6:25–34. What specific things does Jesus tell us not to worry about (v. 25)?

Drink, food, clothing, tomorrow

3. How do people demonstrate their worry about physical needs? (Be specific.) *Borrow money*
Run up debts. Save?

4. In what specific areas do you have trouble obeying this command to not worry? Why?

Safety of nearest & dearest
Health problems. Meeting deadlines
eg service prep.

5. How should the fact that God feeds the birds and clothes the flowers affect our concern about food and clothes (vv. 26, 28–30)?

If we simplify our needs, God
does provide eg. clothes - if needed,
in charity shops etc.

6. Why is worrying about our physical and material needs an affront to God?

*Betrays a lack of trust,
On other hand idleness is too,*

7. When we make our physical and material needs our primary focus in life, how are we acting like pagans (vv. 31–32)?

*Got our priorities wrong –
Christns. are pilgrims – not here to amass wealth.*

8. What does it mean to seek God's kingdom and his righteousness (v. 33)? (Give two or three practical examples.)

*To work for Christ – not to better our worldly position.
Spend our time & resources on God's work
– extreme example – mission field.
Giving to charity.*

9. Why is seeking God's kingdom and righteousness the best way to satisfy our spiritual and physical needs (v. 33)?

*There is only 1 way to find lasting joy that is in a life of service.
Choice of work – of Ministry will work in a casino!*

10. Just when Jesus seems to have finished his teaching, he gives one final command: "Do not worry about tomorrow" (v. 34). Why is this good advice?

Cant do anything to change what will happen – only do own preparation.

11. What does this passage teach you about your heavenly Father? *He is loving, generous & wants to care for us.*

12. Take time now to commit your needs to God in prayer. Ask him to help you trust him rather than worrying about those needs. Pray that you will be able to focus more of your time and energy on God's kingdom and his righteousness.

Memory Verse

Seek first his kingdom and his righteousness, and all these things will be given to you as well.

Matthew 6:33

■ BETWEEN STUDIES ■

What changes do you need to make in your attitudes toward physical and material needs? What practical steps will you take to make these changes?

If you have been worried, confess your worry as sin. Talk to God about your needs, asking him to help you distinguish between genuine needs and wants. Then praise him that he is the Good Provider who will give you everything you need (not necessarily everything you want). Finally, focus your attention on obeying God and doing his work. Practice giving him the priority in specific ways this week.

If you are studying in a group, prepare to report at your next meeting what happened during the week.

3

Our Riches In Christ

Ephesians 1:3-14

Seventy years ago, a number of successful financiers met in Chicago. Among them were Charles Schwab, president of the world's largest independent steel company; Richard Whitney, president of the New York Stock Exchange; Albert Fall, a member of President Calvin Coolidge's cabinet; Leon Frasier, president of the Bank of International Settlements; and Ivar Kreuger, head of the world's greatest monopoly. Within twenty-five years, one was broke, two were imprisoned, and two committed suicide.

By the world's standards, they once were very wealthy. But they lost sight of the greatest riches available to them. You may never reach their level financially, but God's blessings described in Ephesians 1 are worth far more.

1. Why do people want to have a lot of money?

Security, Power. Indulgence (self.)

2. Read Ephesians 1:3–14. Paul says that God "has blessed us ... with every spiritual blessing in Christ" (v. 3). What are some of the spiritual blessings Paul mentions in verses 4–14?

Sons. To be free of guilt. Given Jesus
Acceptance at last
Everything wks. for good for us.
Gift of Holy Spirit.
inheritance

3. How many times does Paul use the phrases "in Christ" or "in him" or their equivalent in this passage? *10*

Why is this significant? *Gospel,*

4. How do our spiritual blessings find their source in the eternal love and purposes of God (vv. 4–5)?

God's plan. Sent Jesus.

Helen's

For what purposes did God choose and predestine us?

To bring all things under Christ

5. How do you respond to the fact that God views you as "holy and blameless" in Christ and that he has adopted you as his child (vv. 4–5)?

takes a lot of living up to. my behaviour matters

6. The word "redemption" (v. 7) means to purchase someone out of slavery. "Forgiveness" (v. 7) means to cancel an obligation, a punishment, or guilt. How do these word pictures help you understand God's lavish grace to us in Christ?

The vast importance of it – others think it an insignificant matter –

7. Paul tells us that God has also "made known to us the mystery of his will" (vv. 9–10). What do we learn from these verses about God's ultimate plan for the universe?

it will be brought under control

What can we do now to cooperate with that plan and to bring it to completion?

Pray – listen to H.S. – use our will to carry out God's plan – not our own desires

8. The Holy Spirit is described as a "seal" (a mark of ownership) and "a deposit" (vv. 13–14). What do these words reveal about the significance of the Holy Spirit in our lives?

Because we can know the Spirit we need not feel 'on our own'.

9. The Holy Spirit guarantees our inheritance (v. 14). What images come to mind when you think of your future inheritance in Christ?

10. For the third time Paul mentions the phrase "to the praise of his glory" (vv. 6, 12, 14). What does it mean to praise God's glory and grace?

Bend our minds & focus on His action not our self

How does what God has done for you in Christ make you want to praise him?

Gratitude - awareness of need.

11. In what specific ways can we show God our appreciation for God's blessings by living "to the praise of his glory"?

Work at it - open our minds Practice prayer - seek the 'good' of others.

Memory Verse

Praise be to the God and Father of our Lord Jesus Christ, who has blessed us in the heavenly realms with every spiritual blessing in Christ.

Ephesians 1:3

BETWEEN STUDIES

Think of one area in which your lifestyle is not bringing praise to God. Then list several practical ways to turn this situation around. Pray daily for God's help to do so.

If you are studying in a group, prepare to report your progress at your next meeting.

4

Everything We Need

2 Peter 1:2–11

People frequently confuse needs with desires. We "need" a home in the suburbs, two cars, three weeks of paid vacation, a color television, and designer clothes. We "need" new kitchen cabinets, a new set of golf clubs, and a new stereo system—even though the old ones work fine. Magazine ads and TV commercials make sure that we always "need" more than we have, and we do our best to believe their messages. No wonder we have become one of the most self-indulgent generations in history.

God doesn't give us everything we want, but he always gives us everything we need. Yet in 2 Peter 1:2–11 we discover that when our true needs are met we also receive what our hearts desire most.

1. Why do you think people's desire for "something more" never seems to be satisfied?

Peer pressure. Advertising, Greed, Status.

2. Read 2 Peter 1:2–11. According to Peter, what gifts has God given to every Christian (vv. 3–4)?

Participate in divine nature & escape evil desires.

3. In what sense does our knowledge of God give us "everything we need" (v. 3)?

allows us to add goodness, knowledge self-control etc,

4. Peter tells us that God has given us "very great and precious promises" (v. 4). What are some of the promises that Peter may have in mind?

live life of service to God which is the aim of Chr. life & the guarantee of life in His K'dom,

5. These promises enable us to "participate in the divine nature" (v. 4). What does that mean?

To become more Christlike as we go

6. How can these promises also help us to "escape the corruption in the world caused by evil desires" (v. 4)?

God provides His strength & helps to those who commit their lives; cannot fail

7. Peter tells us to make every effort to add seven qualities to our faith (vv. 5–7). How would you define each of these qualities?

Steps in becoming conformed to Christ's likeness aided by His Spirit.

8. What progression do you see in these qualities?

Start with changing the self & relationship with others

What is significant about this progression?

Means growth.

9. Describe some specific changes in your attitudes, words, and lifestyle that would result from obeying these commands.

Attitude to other people. I tend to criticize, know best & want to change them - ought to let God do changing

31

10. What is God's part in developing these qualities of a healthy Christian life?

If we start He will help.

What is your part?

Trust, Prayer, Confession, Study,

11. How does possessing these qualities in increasing measure enable us to be effective and productive as Christians (v. 8)?

Object is to serve others & so serve God. Need to train to do that.

12. What can we conclude about those who lack these qualities (v. 9)?

They haven't made any committment

13. What promise does God give to those who obey verses 5–10?

We become effective & productive —

What is special about this promise for you?

Don't want to be ineffective & unproductive. Must not mistake reliance of human strength for God's given qualities.

Memory Verse

His divine power has given us everything we need for life and godliness through our knowledge of him who called us by his own glory and goodness.

1 Peter 1:3

■ BETWEEN STUDIES ■

In the chart below, list the seven qualities Peter said we should add to our faith. Next to each one, prayerfully rate yourself on a scale of 1 to 10 (10 is the highest). How would your spouse/roommate/friend rate you? (If you're feeling brave, ask that person instead of guessing!) Then choose one quality with a low rating, and circle it. Identify a couple of specific steps you can take to increase it in your life. Don't forget to ask God to help you follow through.

If you are studying in a group, prepare to report your progress at your next meeting.

Character Qualities	Score from 1–10

5

Gifts of the Spirit

1 Corinthians 12

When Mary, the queen of Scotland, visited Balmoral Castle in the summer, she walked around the area without a guard or escort. Most of the people knew her by sight. But one day she had walked further away from the castle than normal. When the sky darkened, she knocked on a door to see if she could borrow an umbrella.

The lady who answered did not recognize the queen and hesitated to lend her good umbrella to a stranger, afraid she would never get it back. So she dug up an old broken one with holes. Apologizing for its condition, she gave it to the queen.

The following day, another stranger knocked on the lady's door. A man handed her an envelope, stating that the queen had sent him to express her thanks for the umbrella.

When the woman realized what had happened, she was ashamed and muttered, "Had I known it was the queen, I'd have given her my best!"

God has given us great gifts to share with others. But are we giving them our best or our leftovers?

1. When you receive a gift, what do you usually do with it? Why? *Put it in an appropriate place - eg. to look at, to eat, to read.*

2. Read 1 Corinthians 12:1–11. Why do you think Paul doesn't want us to be ignorant about spiritual gifts (v. 1)? *If we have a gift it should be used for the good of the church.*

3. How are the various spiritual gifts in the church different and similar (vv. 4–6)? *Differ - not every-one can use same gift. Similar - they all contribute to the growth of the church.*

4. How and why does God give each believer at least one spiritual gift (vv. 7–11)? *So each can contribute to the life of the church. How?*

5. Describe how one or more of the gifts Paul mentions might be used "for the common good" of the church (vv. 7–11). *Wisdom - not cleverness but a closeness to God that God can make His will known - it's what we seek in group prayer. Prophecy - make God's teaching known (like preacher Between Spirits - what is of God & what of devil*

6. Read verses 12–31. Why is Paul's comparison of the body of Christ to a human body a good analogy?

Makes it clear how ea. can contribute to growth of whole church.

7. How can we encourage those who feel they are useless or who are envious of the gifts of others (vv. 14–20)?

Help them to pray – not give God a 'shopping list' – but allow God into the secret places of the heart = to confess –

8. What do those who feel superior and self-sufficient fail to realize about themselves and others (vv. 21–26)?

Whatever gift they have was given for benefit of all – they also need the help the holders of other gifts can provide –

9. With which group do you identify most: those who feel useless and envious or those who feel superior and self-sufficient? Explain.

– temptation to feeling of superiority – but I know my limitations in life & church –

How can Paul's statements about the body give you a more balanced perspective about yourself and others?

Learn to see gifts in others & respect & encourage their gifts

10. How can we use our spiritual gifts to promote unity in a group of believers, such as a study group or congregation?

Recog. it's not our cleverness or skill but God's gift - like any other attribute can't claim any credit - encourage others.

11. What additional gifts does Paul mention in 27–28?

Apostles, Teachers, miracle workers, helpers, administrative gifts.

12. When you compare the two lists in this chapter (see also Rom. 12:6–8), which gifts do you feel God has given you?

Serving

Teaching & preaching (prophecy some admin. gifts.

Give examples of how you might use these gifts to serve others in the body of Christ.

Teach & preach in church (at one time in school & youth work. Admin = property steward.

13. What do you learn about God our good provider from this chapter?

God provides what is needed to build up His Church. We don't always apply them nor recognize others' gifts

Memory Verse

Each one should use whatever gift he has received to serve others, faithfully administering God's grace in its various forms.

1 Peter 4:10

■ BETWEEN STUDIES ■

How are you using the spiritual gifts you received from God? In what specific ways are you building up Christ's body because you're exercising your gifts?

If you don't know what gifts God has given you, begin the process of finding out. There are several excellent books available to guide you in understanding the gifts mentioned in the New Testament and in determining yours. Look for one of the following to get started: *Discover Your God-Given Gifts* by Don and Katie Fortune (Chosen/Baker Books, 1987); *19 Gifts of the Spirit* by Leslie B. Flynn (Victor Books, 1974); *Unwrap Your Spiritual Gifts* by Kenneth O. Gangel (Victor Books, 1983); *Discovering Your Spiritual Gifts: A Personal Inventory Method* by Kenneth C. Kinghorn (Zondervan, 1984).

6

The Best Is Yet to Come

Revelation 21:1–22:6

In speculating about heaven, Billy Graham wrote:

> What is heaven going to be like? Just as there is a mystery to hell, so there is a mystery to heaven. Yet I believe the Bible teaches that heaven is a literal place. Is it one of the stars? I don't know. I can't even speculate. The Bible doesn't inform us. I believe that out there in space where there are one thousand million galaxies, each a hundred thousand light years or more in diameter, God can find some place to put us in heaven. I'm not worried about where it is. I know it is going to be where Jesus is. Christians don't have to go around discouraged and despondent with their shoulders bent. Think of it—the joy, the peace, the sense of forgiveness that He gives you, and then heaven too.

Yes, think about it. God has given us so many wonderful gifts to enjoy. But when our time on earth is done, he will keep on giving to us. And the best is yet to come.

1. When you were a child, how difficult was it for you to wait until your birthday or Christmas to open your gifts? Why?

2. Read Revelation 21:1–8. What do you learn about our future home from John's description in verses 1–7?

   What appeals to you most about this description?

3. Who won't be with God in the future (v. 8)? Why?

4. Read 21:9–27. Why do you think John goes into such great detail as he describes the New Jerusalem?

5. What is outstanding or noteworthy to you about John's description of the city? Why?

6. Why do you think John mentions again who will and who will not inhabit this city (v. 27)?

7. Read Revelation 22:1–6. How is the city described here similar to the Garden of Eden (see Gen. 2:8–14)?

8. In what ways does the city far exceed the Garden of Eden and differ from it?

9. What brief glimpses do we get of our daily life and activities in the city (22:3–5; see also 21:6–7, 22–27)?

10. John says that we will serve God and see his face (22:3–4). In what ways can you make these a more important part of your daily life now?

11. What are you looking forward to the most in your future residence? Why?

12. What have you learned from this passage about the God you will live with, worship, and serve throughout eternity?

Memory Verse

What kind of people ought you to be? You ought to live holy and godly lives as you look forward to the day of God and speed its coming.

2 Peter 3:11–12

BETWEEN STUDIES

Yes, the best is yet to come. But the thought of living forever with God should motivate us to become more like him, "to live holy and godly lives" as Peter wrote (2 Pet. 3:11). What are you doing to get ready for eternity? Set aside a block of time as soon as possible to evaluate your spiritual life. Set specific goals to increase your godliness, and break them down into measurable steps. Then act on them.

Also take time to praise God for being a good provider. Thank him for his good gifts, especially the ones on which you focused in this study.

Leader's Notes

Leading a Bible discussion—especially for the first time—can make you feel both nervous and excited. If you are nervous, realize that you are in good company. Many biblical leaders, such as Moses, Joshua, and the apostle Paul, felt nervous and inadequate to lead others (see, for example, 1 Cor. 2:3). Yet God's grace was sufficient for them, just as it will be for you.

Some excitement is also natural. Your leadership is a gift to the others in the group. Keep in mind, however, that other group members also share responsibility for the group. Your role is simply to stimulate discussion by asking questions and encouraging people to respond. The suggestions listed below can help you to be an effective leader.

PREPARING TO LEAD

1. Ask God to help you understand and apply the passage to your own life. Unless that happens, you will not be prepared to lead others.

2. Carefully work through each question in the study guide. Meditate and reflect on the passage as you formulate your answers.

3. Familiarize yourself with the leader's notes for the study. These will help you understand the purpose of the study

and will provide valuable information about the questions in the study.

4. Pray for the various members of the group. Ask God to use these studies to make you better disciples of Jesus Christ.

5. Before the first meeting, make sure each person has a study guide. Encourage them to prepare beforehand for each study.

LEADING THE STUDY

1. Begin the study on time. If people realize that the study begins on schedule, they will work harder to arrive on time.

2. At the beginning of your first time together, explain that these studies are designed to be discussions, not lectures. Encourage everyone to participate, but realize that some may be hesitant to speak during the first few sessions.

3. Read the introductory paragraph at the beginning of the discussion. This will orient the group to the passage being studied.

4. Read the passage aloud. You may choose to do this yourself, or you might ask for volunteers.

5. The questions in the guide are designed to be used just as they are written. If you wish, you may simply read each one aloud to the group. Or you may prefer to express them in your own words. Unnecessary rewording of the questions, however, is not recommended.

6. Don't be afraid of silence. People in the group may need time to think before responding.

7. Avoid answering your own questions. If necessary, rephrase a question until it is clearly understood. Even an eager group will quickly become passive and silent if they think the leader will do most of the talking.

8. Encourage more than one answer to each question. Ask, "What do the rest of you think?" or "Anyone else?" until several people have had a chance to respond.

9. Try to be affirming whenever possible. Let people know you appreciate their insights into the passage.

10. Never reject an answer. If it is clearly wrong, ask, "Which verse led you to that conclusion?" Or let the group handle the problem by asking them what they think about the question.

11. Avoid going off on tangents. If people wander off course, gently bring them back to the passage being considered.

12. Conclude your time together with conversational prayer. Ask God to help you apply those things that you learned in the study.

13. End on time. This will be easier if you control the pace of the discussion by not spending too much time on some questions or too little on others.

Many more suggestions and helps are found in the book *Leading Bible Discussions* (InterVarsity Press). Reading it would be well worth your time.

STUDY ONE

Remembering God's Goodness
PSALM 103

Purpose: To praise God for the benefits he has freely given us.

Question 1 Every study begins with a "warm-up question," which is discussed *before* reading the passage. A warm-up question is designed to do three things.

First, it helps to break the ice. Because a warm-up question doesn't require any knowledge of the passage or any special preparation, it can get people talking and can help them to feel more comfortable with each other.

Second, a warm-up question can motivate people to study the passage at hand. At the beginning of the study, people in the group aren't necessarily ready to jump into the world of the Bible. Their minds may be on other things (their kids, a problem at work, an upcoming meeting) that have nothing to do with the study. A warm-up question can capture their interest and draw them into the discussion by raising important issues related to the study. The question becomes a bridge between their personal lives and the answers found in Scripture.

Third, a good warm-up question can reveal where people's thoughts or feelings need to be transformed by Scripture. That is why it is important to ask the warm-up question *before* reading the passage. The passage might inhibit the spontaneous, honest answers people might have given, because they feel compelled to give biblical answers. The warm-up question allows them to compare their personal thoughts and feelings with what they later discover in Scripture.

Question 2 E. Calvin Beisner offers this definition of praise:

> What is it to praise God? Quite simply, it is to speak well of him, to laud him, to boast of him before others. Or, as one person put it, it is ". . . to declare to all about us, as loudly as we can, the goodness and grace of his conduct towards men, and our infinite obligations for all our enjoyments to him. . . ." And that is precisely what David does throughout this whole psalm, all of which is dedicated to reciting God's praiseworthy nature and works" (*Psalms of Promise* [Colorado Springs, Colo.: NavPress, 1988], 198–99; quote is from William Dunlop, cited by Charles Spurgeon, *The Treasury of David,* vol. 2, pt. 2, p. 285).

Note that David praised God with his inner self, not just an outward show. His praise was with his whole being. "Soul" equals mind and heart. "All my inmost being" refers to his mind, heart, will, and emotions. You may want to spend a few minutes discussing specific ways we can praise God with our souls versus praising him with outward motions.

Question 3 Consider E. Calvin Beisner's comments on the order of these personal benefits:

> It is no accident that the first of these is forgiveness of sin (v. 3). So long as sin remains unforgiven, God and man are enemies (Ro. 5:9–11). The barrier of sin must be removed before the great blessings of God can come upon us—or rather, since some of God's blessings come on the just and the unjust alike (Mt. 5:45)—before we can recognize them and praise him for them. But once sins are forgiven, the way is clear for God to rain on us many more blessings, including healing (Ps. 103:3), preservation of life (v. 4), and making us loving and compassionate (v. 4)—

in short, all godly desires (v. 5; see also Mt. 6:33) (*Psalms of Promise*, p. 197).

Don't let your group get sidetracked on the benefit of healing. Depending on their theological bents, group members may argue that the phrase "heals all your diseases" means we can expect healing for all diseases now. But this psalm may imply healing in the future, after our life on earth, when all diseases will be eliminated and our bodies will be perfect.

Question 4 If you have time, ask each group member to share one experience. If not, ask several volunteers to do so.

David mentioned three conditions for receiving God's benefits: fearing God (vv. 11, 13, 17), keeping his covenant (v. 18), and obeying his precepts (v. 18).

To fear God means to reverence him, to hold him in awe (like viewing the Grand Canyon or Rocky Mountains), to want to please him. Keeping his covenant refers to being faithful to God, which involves obedience to his commands; see Deuteronomy 6:1–15 and 7:6–11. Precepts are responsibilities.

Question 9 Allow adequate time to discuss this question. It is designed to focus your attention on God who is the source of the benefits described in this psalm.

Question 10 Eugene Peterson compares this celebration of praise to a heavenly orchestra:

> In order to get the full impact of these verses, encourage the group to use their imagination. Try to picture the mighty angels in one section of the orchestra, the heavenly hosts (countless multitudes) in another, all other created beings and things in another, and the psalmist standing in the conductor's place. With sweeping gestures, he draws out notes of praise first from one section then another, until the entire creation—including the psalmist—is praising and worshiping the Lord. This is an overpowering scene! (*Psalms: Prayers of the Heart* [Downers Grove, Ill.: InterVarsity Press, 1987], p. 57).

Why We Shouldn't Worry

MATTHEW 6:25–34

Purpose: To stop worrying about physical needs by putting God first and trusting him to provide.

Question 2 The Greek word for "worry" means to be distracted or drawn in different directions, to be anxious about something. The word therefore indicates that we should not worry because God is our master (assuming he is). He is in control and can take care of our needs.

Question 4 Encourage group members to open up by sharing an area you tend to worry about.

Question 7 "The word 'pagans' refers to those who do not know God. Those who have no hope in God naturally put their hope and expectations in things they can enjoy now. They have nothing to live for but the present, and their materialism is perfectly consistent with their religion. They have no God to supply their physical or their spiritual needs, their present or their eternal needs, so anything they get they must get for themselves. They are ignorant of God's supply and have no claim on it. No heavenly Father cares for them, so there is reason to worry" (John MacArthur, Jr., *The MacArthur New Testament Commentary, Matthew 1–7* [Chicago: Moody Press, 1985], p. 425).

Worrying about having needs fulfilled is a denial of trust in God. Worriers might as well be pagans who don't belong to God.

Question 8 God's kingdom is his sovereign rule, his will, his authority. God's righteousness is his holiness that he wants us to emulate (1 Pet. 1:15).

You may want to ask each group member to give an example. Don't be content with vague answers, such as "put God first." Push for more specific examples, such as including a daily quiet time in my list of priorities and then keeping it.

Our Riches in Christ
EPHESIANS 1:3–14

Purpose: To show God our appreciation of his blessings in salvation by living to bring praise to him.

Question 2 Spiritual blessings are "those blessings relating to the believer's new nature and position" (Homer A. Kent, Jr., *Ephesians: The Glory of the Church* [Chicago: Moody Press, 1971], p. 19). They pertain to our relationship with Christ.

Question 3 "The sphere within which the divine blessing is bestowed and received is the Lord Jesus Christ. In the first fourteen verses of the Ephesian letter Jesus Christ is mentioned either by name or title . . . no fewer than fifteen times. And the phrase 'in Christ' or 'in him' occurs eleven times" (John R. W. Stott, *The Message of Ephesians*, The Bible Speaks Today [Downers Grove, Ill.: InterVarsity Press, 1979], p. 34).

Question 4 Don't let group members argue over the ideas of God choosing and predestining us for salvation. If the issue arises, it might be helpful to read the following explanation:

> This sovereign act of God chose some to experience the blessings of salvation. The reasons or criteria for his choice have not been told to us, except that it was according to his own good pleasure (1:9). The fact of a chosen group was well known to Jews, from the Old Testament (Deut. 4:37; 7:6–8; Isa. 41:8), but now it is revealed that God's election in the church includes Gentiles also (Kent, *Ephesians*, p. 20).

God's adoption of us places us in his family as adults after being born again.

> Adoption is the act of God by which he gives his 'born ones' an adult standing in the family. Why does he do this? So that we might immediately begin to claim our inheritance and enjoy our spiritual wealth! A baby cannot legally use this inheritance (Gal. 4:1–7), but an adult son can—and should! This means that you do not have to wait until you are an old saint before you can claim your riches in Christ (Warren W. Wiersbe, *Be Rich* [Wheaton, Ill.: Victor Books, 1976], p. 19).

Finally, God accepted us since he freely gave us what we don't deserve.

Questions 6–7 According to verses 7–10, God did three things for us in Christ. First he redeemed us. Christ's death on the cross paid the price for our freedom from slavery to sin. Second, he forgave us because of his Son's death on the cross. Third, he made known to us the mystery of his will—that he will eventually bring everything together in Christ.

Question 8 The Spirit seals us and acts as a deposit. Sealing a letter, document, package of goods, or product indicated a finished transaction, ownership, security, or protection. The Spirit does all of these for believers. As a deposit, his indwelling is a down payment to guarantee the final purchase, that God will finish his work in us and take us to live with him for eternity.

Questions 10–11 When we live to "the praise of his glory," we live according to God's Word, demonstrating the fact that we belong to God.

> In one sense we give God glory when we recognize his presence and praise him for the qualities his acts unveil. . . . But there is another New Testament sense in which we give God glory. Jesus spoke of his own actions as bringing glory to God (John 14:13) and called on his disciples to bear fruit to the "Father's glory" (John 15:8). . . . Because God is present in believers today, he is able to display his qualities in our lives and so to glorify himself in us (Lawrence O. Richards, *Expository Dictionary of Bible Words* [Grand Rapids, Mich.: Zondervan, 1985], p. 311).

STUDY FOUR
Everything We Need
2 PETER 1:2–11

Purpose: To recognize that God has already given us everything we need as believers and to cooperate with him so that we can grow in Christ.

Questions 3–4 Push group members to identify specific illustrations of "everything we need for life and godliness" and specific promises of God. To reinforce the importance of Peter's teaching in these verses, read the following comments:

> When you are born into the family of God by faith in Christ, you are born complete. God gives you everything you will ever need "for life and godliness." Nothing has to be added! "And ye are

complete in him" (Col. 2:10). The false teachers claimed that they had a "special doctrine" that would add something to the lives of Peter's readers, but Peter knew that nothing could be added. Just as a normal baby is born with all the "equipment" he needs for life and only needs to grow, so the Christian has all that is needed and only needs to grow. God never has to call back any of his "models" because something is lacking or faulty (Warren W. Wiersbe, *Be Alert* [Wheaton, Ill.: Victor Books, 1984], pp. 11–12).

Questions 7–8 "The English word *add* does not adequately express the meaning of the Greek. Used of an individual who underwrote the expenses of the choruses in Greek plays, the word came to mean 'generous and costly cooperation.' Thus Peter implies that the Christian ought to willingly and actively cooperate with God in order to produce the Christian life" (Louis A. Barbieri, *First and Second Peter* [Chicago: Moody Press, 1977], p. 97).

Emphasize that spiritual growth isn't automatic. We can't shift into autopilot once we come to know the Lord; we need to work with him to become more like him.

Be sure group members understand that the faith on which these other qualities are built refers to saving faith. We cannot experience growth in these qualities until we have a personal relationship with God through faith in Christ.

The seven qualities Peter mentions may be briefly defined as follows:

Goodness: Moral excellencies; doing what is right as well as not doing what is wrong.

Knowledge: Practical knowledge, discernment.

Self-control: Control of passions instead of being controlled by them.

Perseverance: Patiently enduring difficulties and pressures. It is learned primarily in trials (James 1:2–8).

Godliness: Likeness to God, seeking to please him.

Brotherly kindness: Warm-hearted affection for others in the body of Christ.

Love: Unselfishly giving of yourself and your best to help others whether or not they deserve it or even respond; genuine care demonstrated by actions.

Question 9 If group members are slow to respond to this question, encourage them by sharing a change you have seen in yourself.

Question 10 Philippians 2:12–13 helps to explain this question. Ask a volunteer to read these verses aloud.

Questions 11–13 Warren Wiersbe, in his commentary on 2 Peter (*Be Alert,* pp. 18–19), states that verses 8–11 give three evidences of spiritual growth: fruitfulness (v. 8), vision (that is, a lack of spiritual nearsightedness) (v. 9), and security (vv. 10–11).

STUDY FIVE	*Gifts of the Spirit*
	1 CORINTHIANS 12

Purpose: To understand that God has given each believer at least one spiritual gift to use for building up the body.

Question 2 John MacArthur, Jr. defines spiritual gifts as "special capacities bestowed on believers to equip them to minister supernaturally to others, especially to each other" (*The MacArthur New Testament Commentary: 1 Corinthians* [Moody Press, 1984], p. 290). They are not the same as natural talents and abilities since they are supernaturally given when a person becomes a Christian.

Don't let group members get sidetracked on controversial issues associated with spiritual gifts. Keep them focused on the text and the discussion questions.

Question 3 In these verses Paul emphasizes both the diversity and the unity within the body of Christ. He mentions three areas in which Christians are different.

First, there are different kinds of "gifts" (v. 4). The word "gifts" comes from the Greek word *charismata* and emphasizes that these gifts are graciously (*charis*) given by God. In fact, the modern Greek word means "a birthday present."

Second, there are different kinds of "service" (v. 5). Spiritual gifts are not given to call attention to ourselves and our special abilities. They are given to us for the express purpose of serving others in the body of Christ.

Third, Paul states that there are different kinds of "workings" (v. 6). David Prior writes, "The Spirit produces results, varied results which can be noticed: changed lives, transformed relationships, increasing congregations, effective testimony, released talents. As each of these is energized by the Spirit, the Lordship of Jesus is demonstrated in as many diverse ways as there are people who possess this energy" (*The Message of 1 Corinthians*, The Bible Speaks Today [Downers Grove, Ill.: InterVarsity Press, 1985], p. 197).

Yet in spite of the diversity within the body of Christ, Paul also emphasizes the unity of the church. The different gifts, kinds of service, and workings are given by "the same Spirit" (v. 4), "the same Lord" (v. 5), and "the same God" (v. 6). The triune God (Father, Son, and Spirit) is involved both in giving the gifts to each of his children and in empowering the ministry of every believer.

Question 4 Be sure everyone understands that God gives us spiritual gifts to help others, not for private edification. Have someone read 1 Peter 4:10 aloud to reinforce this point.

Question 5 You may want to include the list of gifts Paul mentions in verse 28 as part of your discussion of this question. The notes for this passage in *The NIV Study Bible* (Grand Rapids, Mich.: Zondervan, 1985) can also provide you with a helpful definition of each gift.

Question 12 If the members of your group know each other well, you might take time to have them comment on the gifts of others in the group and how God has used those gifts to help them as Christians. This can be a very affirming exercise if it is done properly.

If anyone wants to study gifts in more detail, Ephesians 4:11–13 and 1 Peter 4:10–11 also list specific gifts and why they are given.

The Best Is Yet to Come

REVELATION 21:1—22:6

Purpose: To explore God's gift of living with him forever and to get ready now to receive that gift.

Question 2 Spend a couple of minutes thinking about how wonderful it will be to live with God forever. You may want to ask group members to review how God has dwelt with his people in the past, or read the following comments:

> The most important thing about the city is that God dwells there with his people. The Bible gives an interesting record of the dwelling places of God. First, God walked with man in the Garden of Eden. Then he dwelt with Israel in the tabernacle and later in the temple. When Israel sinned, God had to depart from those dwellings. Later, Jesus Christ came to earth and "tabernacled" among us (John 1:14). Today, God does not live in man-made temples (Acts 7:48–50), but in the bodies of his people (1 Cor. 6:19–20) and in the church (Eph. 2:21–22).
>
> In both the tabernacle and the temple, the veil stood between men and God. That veil was torn in two when Jesus died, thus opening a "new and living way" for God's people (Heb. 10:19ff.). Even though God dwells in believers today by his Spirit, we still have not begun to understand God or fellowship with him as we would like; but one day, we shall dwell in God's presence and enjoy him forever (*Be Victorious* [Wheaton, Ill.: Victor Books, 1985], pp. 146–47).

Questions 3 and 6 Emphasize that those who will not inhabit the new Jerusalem are not occasional sinners in these areas but practice these sins as a lifestyle.

Question 4 Don't try to describe each jewel or attach symbolic meaning to everything in John's vision of the New Jerusalem. Paint a word picture for effect and try to discover the main impression John is seeking to create.

Question 9 John mentioned that we will serve God and reign with him forever. Apparently we won't sit around playing harps!

Question 10 Encourage group members to be specific and practical. Point out that serving God and worshiping him should play an important role in our daily lives now—especially since we will be involved in these activities throughout eternity.

Question 11 Allow enough time for everyone to respond to this question. You may want to go around the circle to be sure each person has an opportunity to share his or her sense of anticipation.

Question 12 After answering this question, broaden it to the whole study guide to review what you have learned about our Good Provider. Then spend a few minutes praising God for being such a good giver and for specific gifts he has given us.

NOTES

NOTES

NOTES

NOTES

NOTES

NOTES

NOTES